Bullying & Harassment
Values and Best Practice Responses

Frank Scott-Lennon
& Margaret Considine

MANAGEMENT BRIEFS

Essential Insights for Busy Managers

Acknowledgements

We are most grateful to the many managers and employees — too numerous to mention - within various organisations; their insights have greatly informed our thinking and our view of Values and Best Practice.

We are also most grateful to those managers who read earlier drafts of this book and who enriched us with their insights.

We are greatly indebted to Andrew Kakabadse, Mary Redmond and Frank Kelly for taking the time to read the book and provide us with such wonderful endorsements.

We particularly wish to thank our spouses, Claire and Hugh, for their continuing support; without it this book, and all of our other work, would be less rich.

Frank Scott-Lennon
Margaret Considine

December 2008

© 2008 Frank Scott-Lennon and Fergus Barry
ISBN 0-9519738-3-5
ISBN 978-0-9519738-3-7

All design, art work and liaison with printers has been undertaken by
Neworld Associates, 9 Greenmount Avenue, Harold's Cross, Dublin 12.

Publisher: Managements Briefs, 30 The Palms, Clonskeagh, Dublin 14.

Table of Contents

Foreword

This book captures the Values that organisations should espouse in respect of Bullying, Harassment and Sexual Harassment. In addition the book deals with many aspects of Best Practice responses to these difficult situations.

It is a very welcome addition to our developing series of Human Resource, Organisation Behaviour and General Management Books, with many more titles to follow.

All of the books in the series aim to capture the essentials for busy managers; essential knowledge and skill presented in an accessible easy-to-read style.

A list of books already published within the series appears on the inside of the back cover; our website www.ManagementBriefs.com lists forthcoming titles.

We welcome any contact from you the reader; it will only improve our products and our connection to our reader population.

Frank Scott-Lennon
Series Editor
frank@ManagementBriefs.com

December 2008

Introduction

1

Chapter outline
Introduction

→ Definitions
→ Dignity and Respect
→ Bullying and Harassment
→ Sexual Harassment
→ Rights of Natural Justice
→ Empowering those feeling bullied
   or harassed
→ Best Practice Responses

Every employee is entitled to have expectations that he/she will be treated with dignity and respect in the workplace. This implies that the behaviour of his/her colleagues and that of management will be such as to pose no challenge to the dignity and respect that is their right. This dignity and respect is due to them not only in the roles which they carry out within the organisation but also as stand alone individuals.

Organisations owe it to their employees to foster a culture of dignity and respect within the organisation through developing and promulgating policies and practices specifically aimed at enhancing such a culture. Every employer should recognise the right of all staff to be treated with dignity & respect at work, and many companies would have a formal Dignity at Work Policy to support this value. This right ensures that all employees are free to do their work in a safe environment which is free from Harassment, Sexual Harassment & Bullying, whether carried out by a member(s) of staff, a customer, a client or a business contact of the employer; this applies to work on the employer's premises, assignments off those premises and to social occasions that are work-related.

Looking at the stated values of many organisations they often cite values such as honesty, equality, diversity, learning and many more – the stating and the living of a value set for an organisation are very different in paper and in practice.

Take Honesty for example: whether manager or employee we all have the right to this in work, particularly if it is a stated and agreed value. However, we also have the responsibility to afford it to others who have that same right.

For every right in an organisation, we have the same responsibilities:

→ If we have the right to be heard we have the responsibility to listen and hear

→ If we have the right to autonomy, we have the responsibility to afford it to staff (relative to their will and skill)

→ If we have the right to be treated with integrity, we have the responsibility to act with integrity ourselves

Panel 1.1

Dignity and respect

Dignity and respect is what all individuals feel when the climate within an organisation is one that takes positive action to support behaviours that contribute to dignity and respect and stamp out those that go against it.

Major challenges to such a culture of dignity and respect arise from Bullying and Harassment (B&H) behaviour which speaks volumes about the individual who perpetrates such behaviour. Such Bullying and Harassment behaviour usually has very little to do with the person it is perpetuated against. Bullying is therefore mostly saying more about the bully than the person being bullied.

The situation has varying levels of effects on the individual who is on the receiving end of such B&H behaviour. Brief definitions of both Bullying & Harassment and Sexual Harassment are shown in Panel 1.2, 1.3 (below) and 1.4 overleaf.

Panel 1.2

A useful working definition of Bullying

Workplace bullying is repeated inappropriate behaviour, direct or indirect, whether verbal, physical or otherwise, conducted by one or more persons against another or others, at the place of work and/or in the course of employment, which could reasonably be regarded as undermining the individual's right to dignity at work. An isolated incident of the behaviour described in this definition may be an affront to dignity at work but as a once-off incident is not considered to be bullying.

Example:
Imogen started work in a reputable financial institution eighteen months ago, passed her probationary review and has had good performance reviews ever since. Recently her reporting line changed and her new manager has a very different style and approach to her previous boss. Her new manger is often rude to her in front of colleagues and at client meetings. Imogen feels that she is being bullied. She asserts that the quality of her work is being questioned in public and held up for ridicule, with statements like, 'I wouldn't have done it like that, this is not up to our professional standard,' or at team meetings, displaying on a LCD screen one of her recent emails to a client as an example of poor business English.

Panel 1.3

Harassment in practice is similar to sexual harassment but on grounds other than gender.

Harassment is a form of discrimination and is normally based on one of the following relevant characteristics of the employee: Marital Status, Family Status, Sexual Orientation, Religious Belief (or none), Age, Disability, Race, Colour, Nationality or ethnic or national origin, or membership of a minority community.

Example:

Brian, an IT specialist knew that his skills were in high demand but after six years abroad, he wanted to return home. He had applied for a good consultancy role with a young progressive company and had conducted three web cam interviews with various levels of their senior management team. He had completed a series of psychometric tests and it was now down to the final two candidates, so he had to travel home for his face-to-face interview. The company paid all the expenses and on the day of the interview his Dad, who had retired early, drove him into Dublin 2 for his interview. At reception, there seemed to be some confusion when he asked for directions to the interview. He was informed that it was on the 4th floor but there was no lift. Brian was in a wheelchair. When Brian asked if he could be interviewed on the ground floor, he was informed that it was not possible as his potential new employer only had the lease of the fourth floor of this Georgian building. He rang his Dad, who returned to the building and who proceeded to carry Brian up the stairs for his interview and then brought his wheelchair up. As they waited Brian saw a friend of his from college emanate from the interview room and they had a short chat. This was the competition, Brian felt comfortable that his knowledge and expertise far outweighed the competition and he did in his mind a good interview, despite the bad start to the day. A week later when he was informed that he didn't get the job, he was convinced that it was because he was disabled.

Sexual harassment is all that we have said above in respect of B&H but with sexual connotations. Sexual harassment also is oftentimes perpetrated in a situation where the offender implies or formally states that the granting of sexual favours will have a beneficial effect on the career of the individual.

Panel 1.4

Sexual Harassment is an Act of physical intimacy that involves:

→ A request for sexual favours

→ Other act or conduct including spoken words, gestures or the production, display or circulation of written words, pictures or other material

That is unwelcome and could reasonably be regarded as sexually orientated or is otherwise on the ground of gender offensive, humiliating or intimidating.

Example:

A group of young graduate trainees — male and female, had spent six weeks on an off-site intensive management development programme and had developed a strong bond of friendship and belonging. At the start of the programme the guys had raided the girls locker room and taken their underwear and replaced them with male underwear. On a team based activity in the last week, all participants had to change and shower between two particular activities in separate changing rooms. Later that evening photos of a number of the ladies in various levels of undress, appeared on the notice board with their heads cut off — with the caption 'Guess who' at the top of the board. It appeared that a number of the men had video footage of this on their mobile phones also. During the rush to change between exercises, someone had thought it was funny to take photos and mobile phone video footage from under the door of the changing room without aim or focus which resulted in the badly framed shots of many of the female trainees. The guys thought it was just another bit of fun and a form of bonding for a team that had been through such a rigorous programme. Each of the females felt terribly violated and sexually harassed and the prospect of working with these male colleagues in the future was intimidating to say the least.

Panel 1.5

Rights of Natural Justice

When a complaint is made of bullying, harassment or sexual harassment — all parties are entitled to the rights of Natural Justice which include:

→ The right to know the complaint made

→ The right to fair examination of same

→ The right of reply

→ The right to be represented

→ The right to due consideration

Bullying & Harassment

Bullying & Harassment is the imposition of one person's will on another through specific aggressive behaviours that threaten the other and leave them feeling undermined and vulnerable. Furthermore B&H trespasses on the freedom of individuals and oftentimes leaves them with feelings of negative well-being; these feelings can be from mild negative well-being to more serious damage to the individual's self-image or health.

> Those who feel bullied should be helped to confront the bully and indicate to her/him those behaviours that are causing offence.

All of the examples cited on the previous page could result in findings of bullying or harassment against the perpetrator(s) – facts and evidence dependent.

There are many causes of B&H type behaviour within organisations but within this introductory set of ideas we will identify just three:

→ Individuals who have a warped sense of how they should deal with people and of the power that they wield; indeed very often the bully is one who sets out to deliberately abuse power in respect of other individuals

→ Bad organisational policies and practices that allow a B&H culture to develop across the organisation or in small units within the organisation

→ Responses from those who are bullied and harassed that leaves the bully with the view that they can 'get away with' their behaviour

The purpose of this guide is primarily twofold. Firstly, to provide practising managers that encounter these negative work practices with insight, approaches, advice and practical strategies for dealing with the issue(s); secondly, a practical resource guide for those that have ever been subjected to these negative practices in their place of work.

Managers faced with the challenge of being the first interventionist need a repertoire of proven tools and techniques that assist and do not escalate the problem; and which give consistency, impartiality and credibility to the process; also techniques that will provide them with a form of professional indemnity due to the fact that they followed best practice in the situation.

One of the principal aims of this book is to provide those who feel bullied and harassed with particular advice as to how they might behave when subjected to the multifarious forms of B&H. In many respects each individual's case requires a response that takes account of the nuances of that case but notwithstanding this it is possible to formulate best practice responses as shown in Panel 1.5 below.

We write this book therefore with a view to:

→ Helping individuals identify and name bullying situations

→ Empowering them with the confidence and skill to take corrective actions

→ Offering practical assistance for such individuals, practising managers and organisations as to best practice in B&H situations

→ Ensuring that personal dignity gets to the forefront of organisational behaviour at all times.

Panel 1.6

Best Practice Responses

→ Those who feel bullied should be helped to confront the bully and indicate to her/ him those behaviours that are causing offence and the feelings that such behaviours leave within the victim

→ If this does not bring about the desired change then the individual should initiate organisational help for a mediated route leading to a full recognition of the current situation and agreement as to respectful values and behaviours for the future

→ In situations where the mediated route has not succeeded one of the parties or the organisation should initiate a formal investigation – although this should only be as a last resort

→ Organisations should ensure that individuals who perceive themselves to be in a B&H situation receive whatever assistance is required from within or outside the organisation. Such assistance should help them in coming to a clear realisation that (in the vast majority of situations) the B&H behaviours that had developed were not of their doing and that they should not in any way blame themselves for same

Summary of Chapter 1

→ Every employee has the right of being treated with dignity and respect

→ Managers within organisations should foster a culture of dignity and respect

→ B & H can occur within the organisation, within related organisations and in social situations related to work

→ Rights to our own dignity and respect also bring responsibilities to treat others with dignity and respect

→ Bullying is a repeated behaviour

→ Harassment is a form of discrimination on particular grounds, such as age or race and need only be one incidence of that behaviour

→ Sexual Harassment is behaviour that states or implies that the granting of sexual favours will have a beneficial effect on another individual's career

→ Those who feel bullied or harassed should be:

  – Empowered to confront the perpetrator
  – Afforded a mediation process
  – Afforded a full investigation, if mediation fails
  – Provided with relevant support

→ This book aims to empower those bullied and to highlight best practice managerial/ organisational responses when an organisation is faced with a bullying and harassment claim

Typical Bullying Behaviour in Organisations

2

Chapter outline
Typical Bullying Behaviour in Organisations

→ Bullies explore and exploit weakness
→ Guises of Bullying
→ Examples of bullying behaviour
  – types of abuse
→ Proactive Managerial Responsibilities
→ Corporate governance
→ Encouraging a 'speaking up' climate

Introduction

It is oftentimes difficult for individuals on the receiving end of what they interpret as B&H behaviours to accurately pinpoint the specific issues/incidents that have given rise to their feelings of being bullied and harassed.

Bullies have a tendency to find a weakness or self-perceived weakness in the person they target, spend time exploring it and they then exploit it in the context they are in — i.e. work; they often expand it because concerted bullying behaviour often builds up over time and during that time they have negated the self-esteem and outer confidence of the person they are bullying. All of this affects the defence mechanisms of the person being bullied and harassed, oftentimes leaving them unable to assert themselves.

Bullies within organisations behave in a manner that:

→ Explores perceived weakness in the person they target

→ Exploits the weakness

→ Expands the weakness

Bullying can occur within peer groups (employees of the same level/grade), from management to staff and from staff to management. There are many guises, methods and forms that bullying can take, including behaviours which may:

→ Humiliate:
Prevent a colleague from speaking by using aggressive and/or obscene language

→ Intimidate:
Physical abuse or threats of abuse

→ Verbal Abuse:
Persistent unwarranted criticism or shouting

→ Victimise:
Manipulation of a colleague's reputation by rumour, gossip, ridicule and/or innuendo

→ Exclude and Isolate:
Social exclusion and isolation from various activities

→ Intrude:
Through pestering, invasion of space, spying, stalking or paying undue negative attention to one individual

→ Give repeated unreasonable assignments or duties, which are obviously unfavourable to one individual

→ Manipulate the nature of the work, for example by withholding information or setting meaningless tasks

→ Give repeated impossible deadlines or impossible tasks, for example that could impair their ability to achieve relevant standards within performance reviews

In our experience some of the most common forms of bullying that occur in organisations are included below:

→ A particularly insidious form of B&H is the undermining of the personal confidence and self-esteem of an employee. Behaviours that give rise to such a dip in self-esteem of the staff member usually take place in a series of small events over time; they can often be masked behind a perceived need on the part of the bully for micro-management of the individual, which micro-management often ends up being badly implemented.

Example

Anastazia was at her wits end. Even she did not recognise the second guessing, nervous person she saw in the mirror every day. Another night with disturbed sleep. Where was her self-confidence gone? It seemed to take her twice as long to do things now than it ever did, she re-read everything prior to sending; she deliberated when asked questions in case she got the answer wrong and she could see people, particularly her peer Jan, looking at her as if she did not deserve to have the position she held.

It all seemed to start when Jan pointed out a different perspective on one of her presentations a few months ago and he seemed to get enjoyment out of making her defend her point of view. In the end they opted for his version and she ended up supporting him on implementing this and since then she seemed to be spiralling downwards in terms of self-confidence.

She often felt him just looking at her when she looked up from her computer and he would smirk at her and it made her self-conscious. He had her inundated with emails – curt ones, very direct and instructional. He enjoyed overloading her with work and often including subtle little critical comments like 'if you can manage to fit in this prioritised project into your chaotic day', or 'please check this before you send it – you have a habit of using poor grammar', or 'please send me the minutes for the project meeting **before** (in bold) you issue them to the team' – implying that he did not trust her to do even a basic administration job without his authorisation.

Then last week at a project meeting of peers, he asked who wanted coffee and she automatically got up to get it for everyone – he laughed. Each morning as she found it harder and harder to get out of bed, she asked herself, what was she doing?

→ Managers and team leaders can very often take the opportunity of complaining about an individual to third parties rather than taking issues up directly with the individual. This type of behaviour oftentimes shows the cowardly side of a bully where they actually do not confront the individual but freely talk around the organisation. This is particularly offensive to the individual if and when they hear of such criticisms from these third parties or other people in the organisation.

→ A further form of bullying in organisations does not necessarily involve manager and team member but involves team members jeering/gibing at one another with what is perhaps intended fun but is ultimately not perceived as such by the person who is the target of such jeering/gibing. Either wittingly or unwittingly we can therefore be very unkind to someone within our group by such behaviour which can lead to feelings of being excluded from the 'in-group'.

→ Covert/overt sexual suggestions can also be implied or directly made by individuals through joke, innuendo or direct suggestion where they aim to take advantage of another in the work situation. Organisations should have specific preventative programmes aimed at preventing the continuation of and/or spread of such behaviour.

→ Many situations can present themselves at work where individuals exercise an inappropriate invasion of space with perceived sexual overtones and which leaves the victim feeling in not-too-nice a space or place.

Example

Khalid was very good at what he did, a financial analyst, always cool, logical, analytical and it allowed him to work the way he liked best, in private – most of the time. One of the users of his information, the Sales Director is always hovering over his desk peering at his screen asking questions about this trend or that trend or the consequences of some variance. Once or twice she even leaned on his shoulder as she was reviewing the information. He feels that she has no idea of appropriate personal space and is unprofessional. He would love to have the courage to tell her.

→ Regularly putting obstacles in the way of the usual collaboration that is required of teamwork in today's organisations; sometimes one can find that such obstacles are put across in an aggressive manner. This may well run against an ethic of teamwork within the organisation and leave the individual feeling that they cannot adequately do their job because of their boss or colleague putting such obstacles in the way.

→ Failing to communicate vital job information in a timely manner is also a form of bullying as it is withholding perhaps a key enabling condition in a job holder's ability to successfully undertake their job; such behaviour leaves individuals feeling out of control.

→ A less obvious form of bullying behaviour in organisations is taking credit for the work of others. Unfortunately such behaviour is seen quite often in organisations. It certainly is a great disservice to an individual to have someone else claim credit for their work, particularly if it happens to be a manager/team leader with whom one should have a trusting relationship, or even thought one already had one!

Example

Within a creative agency that is used to working in teams, all of the team accept that it is the Campaign Director that gets the credit in front of the client; however, yesterday it went a step too far for the team. The last series of creative ideas were critiqued quite seriously by the client and last night everyone on the team worked until 2am to turn it around and get a new set of graphics out to the client. At 9.00 pm the Campaign Director left after he ordered Pizzas for everyone and explained that he could do no more, it was in the hands of the creative people now. The next morning the MD came down and complimented the team on their late night effort and the Campaign Director, stood up, thanked him and said, 'we were all here until 2am, my team would do anything for me, they're great' and then proceeded to walk out of the room with the MD telling him about the new slogan that the client would love and not bothering to mention that the new Copyrighter had come up with it. The team just rolled their eyes to heaven. Typical.

→ Regular impatient outbursts of aggression totally disproportionate to the issue at hand. In a modern organisational environment all outbursts of aggression should be totally prohibited. However, as individuals are human, it may be that some exhibit impatient behaviour from time-to-time. The issue here is that it is most certainly bullying behaviour if they are regular outbursts of an emotional nature. It is important to remember that we always face challenges in work – some might try us - and while we have the right to bring our own personality to work, we do not always have the right to 'impose' our style on those we work with.

→ Correcting/re-directing an individual in an aggressive manner over a period of time. It is obviously part of the job of a manager or team leader to undertake the re-direction of some individuals; however, we are here talking of this being done in an aggressive manner and over an extended period of time. So the real issue therefore is the mode in which the manager/team leader carries out this re-direction. Unskilled managers can very often abuse their position in this regard even making use of organisational systems such as the Performance Management System as an opportunity for aggressive behaviour.

A key objective for us in listing the above indicative behaviours is firstly to allow those that are feeling bullied to name and identify some of the behaviours that they may be experiencing. It is also to indicate to team leaders and managers the types of behaviours in which they or some of their colleagues may be engaging, albeit sometimes unconsciously. It is therefore particularly incumbent on

Managers have collective and individual responsibility to provide a safe working environment for all employees.

individual managers to review their own behaviour in the light of the above and ensure that they do not dishonour those with whom they are working by such behaviours which can lead to their feelings of not being respected.

An area that is often cited as giving rise to claims of Bullying and Harassment is the area of negative performance reviews. For clarity – a manager has the right and the responsibility to give an honest analysis of poor performance, to give constructive criticism and re-directional feedback to enable the employee to achieve the desired outcomes. This 'criticism' may leave some people feeling 'bullied' and while the perspective of the victim and how they feel is important and is considered, a manager has the right to conduct a negative performance review and evaluation. How it is done, is what is most important and if done professionally and appropriately, can mitigate a subsequent claim of bullying.

There is also a major responsibility on organisations (senior managers and HR in particular) to ensure that they firmly stamp out any such behaviours that are taking place in their organisations. Good professional managers can best do this by regularly auditing managerial behaviour across the organisation and ensuring that they foster a culture that recognises dignity at work.

Managers have collective and individual responsibility to provide a safe working environment for all employees. This clearly includes the provision of a workplace that is free from B&H and managers in today's organisations must take this responsibility seriously.

Indeed from a corporate governance viewpoint the board of an organisation must be satisfied that such a safe environment exists. Many boards nowadays take a very direct interest in these matters through their Remuneration and HR Committees. These committees can work with management in a collaborative manner to assess behaviour across the organisation in respect of B&H, among other people management issues.

It is important that bullying must be more than a single incident to be considered bullying and that it can occur not just in work or in the course of employment. Also included for consideration are bullying behaviours outside the workplace, work related social activities or on work related activities away from base, all of which should be considered in the same way as workplace incidents.

Organisations do also need to provide support for the development of a 'speaking up' climate and we will turn our attention to this aspect of coping with bullying behaviour in chapter 4 where we handle victim perspectives and feelings.

In the chapter immediately ahead, Chapter 3, we will turn our attention to Harassment and Sexual Harassment.

Summary of Chapter 2

→ Bullies try to capitalise on a weakness that they perceive in the other person

→ Bullying can affect the other person's defence mechanisms

→ Bullying situations can occur between a manager and team member and also between colleagues

→ Sample bullying behaviours include:

- Correcting an individual in an aggressive manner
- Undermining personal confidence and self-esteem
- Complaining about an individual to third parties
- Unwanted jeering and jibing between colleagues
- Covert/overt sexual suggestion
- Taking credit for the work of others
- Impatient outbursts of aggression
- Not communicating vital job information
- Regularly imposing obstacles
- Unprofessional and inappropriate behaviour at performance reviews

→ Organisations have a responsibility to stamp out such behaviours

→ Managers must take seriously their task of providing a safe and healthy environment at work, including one free from Bullying and Harassment

→ Boards, from a corporate governance viewpoint, should take an interest in Bullying and Harassment and other related areas of HR

Harassment &
Sexual Harassment

Chapter outline
Harassment & Sexual Harassment

→ Possible grounds of Discrimination
→ Harassment mediums and channels
→ Examples of Harassment behaviours
→ Example of Sexual Harassment behaviours

Introduction

In simple terms, Harassment is perceived to derive from action or conduct that is unwelcome to the recipient and could be reasonably regarded as offensive, humiliating or intimidating. Sexual harassment is all of this but with sexual overtones or connotations.

A single incident may constitute harassment or sexual harassment.

Harassment and Sexual Harassment can occur in the course of employment, outside the workplace, on work related social activities or on work related activities away from base; all these should be considered by the employer in the same way as workplace incidents.

Panel 3.1

In many jurisdictions Harassment is most often deemed to be so when it is based on, or perceived to be based on, one of the following relevant characteristics of the employee:

→ Marital Status

→ Family Status

→ Sexual Orientation

→ Religious Belief (or none)

→ Age

→ Disability

→ Race

→ Colour

→ Nationality or ethnic or national origin or membership of a minority community

Harassment can be defined as being:

→ Unwanted conduct that has the purpose or effect of violating a person's dignity and creating an intimidating, hostile, degrading, humiliating or offensive environment for the person

→ The unwanted conduct may consist of acts, requests, spoken words, gestures or the production, display or circulation of written words, pictures or other material

It is important to realise that harassment can occur where the person/employee does not have one of the relevant characteristics listed above but the respondent believes that he/she does and treats them in a manner that constitutes harassment. For example when a man is being harassed for being gay or a woman for being lesbian - whether or not they are so.

Harassment Examples:

→ **Verbal Harassment,** such as jokes, comments, ridicule or songs

→ **Written Harassment,** emails, letters, faxes, text messages or notices

→ **Physical Harassment,** such as jostling, shoving or any form of assault

→ **Intimidatory Harassment** such as gesturing, posturing or threatening poses

→ **Isolation** within a work team or exclusion from work related social activities

Panel 3.2

Example of Harassment

Claudia worked as an administrator with a long history of good service. She had a daughter in college whom she was raising on her own and the job and work life balance suited her perfectly. She moved project units within the organisation a number of times and her latest role was as clerical assistant to a short term team of project mangers, who were working on an eighteen month implementation project on contract with the company.

They were all technical and friends of each other having been hired straight out of college for this project. Claudia often felt left out of their clique, she was twenty years older than most of them and they tended to work and socialise together. Equally, they had a project office separate from her front office in which they 'hot desked' and so she was not privy to much of their banter and fun — and any that she was aware of she found much of it to be unprofessional and inappropriate in an office setting and regularly told them so; she even had to ask them to stop swearing at each other while she was on the phone as an elderly member of the public had overheard a dialogue on the phone with colourful language and had complained.

One day she had reason to go into this project office and to her dismay she found what she thought was an effigy of her, made out of blue tack. It was about eight inches long, moulded similar to her build and had her curly hair clearly modelled on the top of her head, and wrinkles drawn on the scowling face. There were lots of pencil marks in it and two pencils stuck in it as if stabbing it. Claudia was extremely upset and left the office feeling victimised because of her age and her approach to 'proper professional behaviour' in work.

Sexual Harassment

Sexual Harassment is any:

→ Act of physical intimacy

→ Request for sexual favours

→ Other act or conduct including spoken words, gestures or the production, display or circulation of written words, pictures or other material

Typical examples of behaviours that could be considered include:

→ **Physical Conduct of a sexual nature:**
This may include unwanted physical contact such as unnecessary touching, patting, pinching, brushing against another person's body, assault or coercive sexual favours.

→ **Verbal Conduct of a sexual nature:**
This may include unwelcome sexual advances, propositions or pressure for sexual activity, continued suggestions at work for social activity outside the workplace after it has been made clear that such suggestions are unwelcome, unwarranted or offensive flirtations, suggestive remarks, innuendoes or lewd comments.

Panel 3.3

Example of Verbal Sexual Harassment

While working in a client's office on a consultancy review with a team of the practice's best consultants, the lead consultant John was subjected to a number of sexual overtones by one of the client's receptionists. It had started off as tame praise, 'you look well today', 'nice suit', 'great smile', 'you must be in good humour today' etc.; however, recently it had become very targeted and explicit.

John had been polite and had not reacted to any of the praise in anything other than what he deemed to be professional appropriateness and in conversation had mentioned that he had a long standing girl friend. He assumed the issue had gone away until his visit last week, when he was in the clients office and the receptionist had said to him that he had seen John's girlfriend (which John could not imagine how this could have happened) and knew who his competition was and was not worried.

The receptionist, Justin, told John that he should explore his true sexuality and admit that he was gay and go out with him instead of his girlfriend. He said this in front of John's full team who were waiting to be shown to a conference room. John was embarrassed and now feels too embarrassed to go back to the client's office and has requested that another project lead be assigned to this client.

→ Non-Verbal Conduct of a sexual nature.
This may include the display of pornographic or sexually suggestive pictures, objects, written materials, emails, text messages or faxes. It may also include behaviour that is suggestive but not verbal, such as leering, whistling or making sexually suggestive gestures.

→ Sex Based Conduct:
This may include conduct that denigrates or ridicules a person or is intimidatory or physically abusive of a person/ employee because of their sex, such as derogatory or denigrating abuse or insults that are gender related.

All of those behaviours described above would be likely to bring about harassment and/or sexual harassment claims. All organisations need to be proactive in creating a culture that precludes such behaviours; and a culture that provides support for individuals subjected to such behaviours

We proceed now to treating Victim Perceptions and Feelings in our next chapter.

Summary of Chapter 3

→ Harassment results from conduct that is unwelcome and could reasonably be regarded as offensive, humiliating or intimidating

→ Sexual Harassment is all of this but with sexual overtones and connotations

→ A single incident may constitute harassment or sexual harassment

→ Harassment can be:

    – Verbal/Written
    – Physical
    – Intimidatory
    – Isolation/Exclusion

→ Sexual Harassment can be:

    – Acts of physical intimacy
    – Verbal conduct of a sexual nature
    – Requests for sexual favours
    – Other acts/gestures
    – Display of words or pictures

27

4

Victim Perspectives and Feelings

Chapter outline
Victim Perspectives and Feelings

→ Understanding Victim perspectives
→ Intention and Impact
→ Understanding intensity of emotions
→ Conflict resolution styles
→ Questioning techniques for
  better understanding

Introduction

We are all a function of what has happened before, in the past; we cannot change that. Our present is an extrapolation of the past, but the future is not; we can shape that. Being able to shape our future is a very good thing for anyone that has suffered at the hands of a bully — for them to be able to rebuild themselves. Equally for any manager faced with resolving conflict between two or more valuable employees; their understanding of how victims feel about it and the effect it has had on them can help the manager understand the needs, interests, fears and concerns of the two parties.

When one party views the incident or conflict from their perspective it always looks right and the same from the other side. We can always see the world from our own perspective and we can be right in our position, from our perspective. However, it might look very different from the other side's perspective. Therefore a harder task is then to see the difficulty and understand it from the perspective of the other party(ies). For a manager faced with understanding it from both sides, that is even harder. Particularly if they are charged with resolving the difficulty – all the more so as either or both parties may regard themselves as the 'victim'.

It is important to move with each person in a particular incident or interaction and walk in their shoes, as it were. One will thus have a good chance of seeing if you can understand how they might feel and through good questioning, listening, attention and rapport techniques figure out why they felt like that.

Six people might be around a table, all right in the position they are holding onto. It takes a brave person to do the right thing as

opposed to being right. They may have to loosen their own position to get behind the position of the other side(s), to see their interests (the reasons they might be holding that position) and most importantly to their needs. It is useful to scratch behind the surface of positions to the interests and needs of the parties and at the needs level one might even find a common ground on which to communicate.

It takes a brave person to do the right thing as opposed to being right.

Intention & Impact are two very different things in reviewing the issue of bullying or harassment. Just because the person complained against did not intend to offend or hurt, does not mean that he or she didn't. It is not intention that is measured but impact on the victim. In reviewing whether a victim was bullied or not the impact on the victim has to be given major consideration. Good questioning techniques, particularly emotion based questions – see Panel 4.1 (right), can help clarify how a victim felt in a given situation.

A simple technique to assist you to understand the impact of how a victim might feel is a technique called emotion mapping. The technique begins with a listing of all of the incidents being spoken of, followed by recording all of the emotions mentioned in relation to a particular element or incident. As none of us are conflict neutral as mediators or managers in attempting to resolve conflict, this helps to prevent one responding with 'Oh, I'd never have felt that, how did he/she react like that', or similar responses. It is important to remember that people subjected to bullying behaviours are often not behaving as they normally would. They are coming from a much lower place in terms of self-confidence and self-esteem. The assertiveness to respond or defend themselves may have been slowly but surely taken away from them by the bully.

To stop a bully, you have to stand up to them - this is dealt with in detail in Chapter 5. That is often the hardest thing to do when you have a victim mentality due to the way you have been treated by the bully. If you don't stand up to the bully just one day, then every day they will affect your life, emotions, self-esteem, confidence, behaviours and actions. Stand up to the bully, you will only have to do it once. Take

---

Panel 4.1

Conflict Resolution Styles

Ask yourself where you stand on the following conflict resolution styles:

→ Are you very competitive, want to win at all costs even for items that are of no real importance to you?

→ Are you so accommodating and nice that you give into the demands of others too easily and don't assert yourself even on things that are very important to you?

→ Do you see every battle as a win/lose, split the size of the pie, 60 for me 40 for you, as a game of compromise?

→ Would you prefer to avoid conflict altogether if you could or do you look on conflict and difference as an opportunity to create something new, to collaborate to find a solution that may not be immediately obvious?

back control of your own life. Believe you can stand up to them. Say 'no' to them once.

All of these styles have their uses in conflict resolution but most of us have a preference for one or two modes which we use repeatedly, because we are good at them. They come naturally to us. We tend to use these styles on which we are reliant whether we actually need that style or not. Thus we can sometimes create as much damage by our attempts to resolve conflict inappropriately as ignoring it all together.

Diagnostic options – a skilled manager might try to move parties in dispute from a rights ("it's my right to go to Court") or positional based ("I'm not working with her again") approach to an interest based approach ("I'm interested in getting justice, equality, fairness, respect... etc.").

This creates options and makes it easier to surface the needs of the parties to the conflict and may even surface some common needs – respect, autonomy, personal development. These can form the basis of a common language that

Panel 4.2

	S Situation	P Problem	E Emotion	N Needs	D Decision
Who?					
Why?					
What?					
Where?					
How?					
When?					

can be used to re-frame the polar perspectives to the conflict and move closer to a resolution. Good questioning techniques have the ability to unlock parties from entrenched positions and move them to talking about what they are interested in order to get their needs addressed. An example of a good questioning framework is displayed in 4.2 on the previous page.

A very important standard to be able to apply for managers is to ask oneself: *"Did I ask similar questions of both sides? Did I record the answers accurately?"*

You can surface all you need to know by asking questions about who, why, what, where, how and when — eg: if you got a complaint or a grievance, who was involved, who witnessed it, why did you respond the way you did, what was actually said, where did it happen, how did it happen, when did it occur.

If you add, the concept SPEND — to it, you can question impartially, consistently and effectively. A very important standard to be

able to apply for managers is to ask oneself: "Did I ask similar questions of both sides? Did I record the answers accurately?" Ask the who why what where how and when questions but with a deeper focus using the SPEND formula. SPEND stands for questions related to Situation, Problem, Emotion, Needs and Decision.

The SPEND framework will help put a structure on one's questioning and help gain insightful knowledge about the complaint — it can be used for gathering relevant information from complainants, respondents and managers dealing with such issues. The framework is best used by working through the who, why, what, where, how and when questions across each letter of the acronym — **S:** Situation, **P:** Problem, **E:** Emotion, **N:** Needs and **D:** Decision. One would use the first three (S, P and E) for gathering the basic information required; following this one would move towards exploring options for solution by continuing the who, why, what, where, how and when questions in respect of N and D.

Summary of Chapter 4

→ We cannot change the past, but we can certainly shape the future

→ It is important to walk in the victim's shoes, so as to fully understand their perspective

→ Intention and Impact are two very different things

→ Understanding one's own conflict resolution styles is important, as is choosing the most appropriate style for the current conflict

→ Attempt to move the parties in dispute from a rights or positional approach to an interest based approach

→ Those bullied and those responding to allegations could benefit from using the SPEND technique of data gathering

5

Standing up
for Oneself

Chapter outline
Standing up for Oneself

→ Providing a climate
→ 5 Assertive steps to 'standing up'
→ Assessing the situation
→ Planning an approach to the bully
→ Confronting the bully in a calm manner
→ Agreeing values to shape subsequent behaviours
→ Reviewing the on-going situation

Introduction

It is extremely important that organisations provide a climate where individuals can feel quite free about standing up for themselves without any fear of further action or victimisation against them. There are, however, varying levels of skill and confidence within individuals in respect of being able to develop an attitude towards standing up and the skills that will help them do so in an assertive manner. Thus one of the proactive actions that an organisation can take in this regard is to provide some form of workshops or add-ons to routine organisational meetings that equip individuals for this 'standing up' process.

As we see it, the **first step** in standing up is the development of an awareness as to what is really happening in a B&H situation, which awareness should lead to an acknowledgement to oneself in the first instance that it is a B&H situation in which one finds oneself. We emphasise this as an initial step because many individuals rather than accurately acknowledging their situation try to continue excusing it; they often do this either by suggesting that the individual did not in fact mean to have them feeling the way they are, or even more insidiously that they themselves are in some way to blame. So it is really important that the individual gets to a point of 'insight' which allows him/her see and acknowledge the current situation sufficiently strongly that it spurs them to taking action.

The **second step** in standing up for oneself is to talk on a confidential basis with some trusted other person, be that a colleague inside the organisation or someone outside. In either event it would be preferable that the individual to whom one would be talking would be familiar with best practice bullying situations or at least be able to point the way towards such experience within another person. The real

---

Panel 5.1

5 assertive steps to 'Standing Up':

→ Assess situation that one is in and fully name it

→ Plan with trusted colleague best means of approach to bully

→ Conduct the conversation with the bully in as calm a manner as possible

→ Agree values that should shape subsequent behaviours

→ Agree to review in the short and medium term how the new arrangements are working benefit of such a conversation is that one can perhaps come to a better understanding of the circumstances surrounding the bullying behaviour and more particularly see a way forward out of the predicament.

The **third step** that one should take is to plan ways in which you might be able to indicate to the bully how unacceptable the behaviour is and to describe the resulting effects of the behaviour on oneself. One may benefit from an on-going conversation with the trusted other person that one has spoken with above, as they may well be able to help out with the sensitivities of planning such an approach.

The **fourth step** would be to carry out the above discussion in as calm a manner as possible but in a way that clearly identifies the unacceptable behaviours and their effect on you. It may be that one needs some mentoring/coaching to be able to carry off such a discussion in as positive a frame of mind as possible. One's behaviour during such a meeting should be aimed at achieving some form of listening on behalf of the bully rather than necessarily having an argument, which is of course easier said than done.

The victim should approach the above meeting with perhaps a limited objective of just getting an understanding that the situation

as she/he feels it actually exists. Therefore they will have a successful meeting if they can bring about some listening on behalf of the perpetrator again to the extent that they will understand the feelings of the victim and develop some joint commitment to creating an alternative working relationship between the two.

The victim should approach the above meeting with perhaps a limited objective of just getting an understanding that the situation as she/he feels it actually exists.

This meeting allows the parties to see the other person's frame of reference for the incident or behaviour. Skilled managers or mediators use re-framing techniques skillfully to move parties off extreme positions (e.g., if it was your daughter/son, would you like someone to say that to her/him). It may well be opportune to adjourn the meeting at this point to allow both sides to reflect on what they have achieved with the concluding focus on a further meeting in a matter of days that will focus on acceptable values and behaviours for the future.

After some days it would then be beneficial to come back together again to allow for a discussion around the kind of values that should determine behaviour between the parties. If they have agreed values it is a very short journey to actually working out what behaviours will follow through from those values and to agree those as the way to behave going forward.

All of what we have described to date should be conducted in as informal a manner as is possible, even though it may be quite a tense situation for all involved. A special effort should be made

Panel 5.2

Typical acceptable values/behaviours

Values	Behaviours
Dignity and respect	Will address each other directly, but in a calm respectful manner, both in private and in public
Support and Review	Will provide support to one another on day-to-day issues and will always review work directly with one another in the first instance
Allocation of credit for work	Will give direct and indirect credit for work done to the party that has undertaken the work
Teamwork	Will provide all necessary collaboration, information and feedback to facilitate optimum team performance
Diversity	Will respect each other's right to be different individually and together seek to find synergies in that difference to enhance a better performance and harmony in the relationship

41

to ensure that the exchanges take place verbally and that nothing is put in writing at this stage between the parties – except perhaps the values and behaviours that are agreed for the future. We say this on the basis that the written word oftentimes appears more harsh than the spoken word and is more difficult to pull back from. The individual who is being bullied and is driving the situation may, however, need to keep a file note for their own personal use of the presenting difficulties, conflict resolution attempts and/or meetings that were held and the basis of any agreement as to future behaviours.

It is also necessary for both parties to agree how they will monitor behaviours in the future and to set a timeframe for same. Such review meetings are an essential part of this process.

If subsequent behaviour is not consistent with the agreement it may be necessary to have a further discussion with the individual and/or chat through one's grievance with another manager, HR or a nominated trusted person in the organisation. It should be noted that many organisations nowadays do have a nominated panel of individuals that can be approached in bullying situations which allows choice to the individual who is feeling victimised.

Panel 5.3

If going to another manager the victim should:

→ If possible, not put anything in writing

→ Clarify what are the offending behaviours, when and how they occurred and their feelings about same

→ Outline resolution efforts to date and the result from same

→ State what one now wants, preferably mediation

→ Agree ways of trying to bring the matter to a mutually satisfactory conclusion

It is preferable that when the complainant brings his/her grievance to another manager they should be encouraged to resist putting the complaint in writing. It is important to try to achieve this because, as mentioned earlier, it will make the ultimate resolution of the grievance more difficult if it has been put into writing. Notwithstanding this caveat if the employee is clearly of the view that they want to put it in writing as their preferred course then they should be permitted so to do.

We will now proceed in Chapter 6 to examine Best Practice Responses for Managers.

Summary of Chapter 5

→ Organisations should take proactive steps to build individual skill and confidence

→ Individuals feeling bullied should first learn to acknowledge that scenario and name it

→ Individuals feeling bullied should:

- Talk on a confidential basis to a colleague/friend
- Plan ways of telling the bully about his/her behaviour and its effect on them
- Conduct such a discussion with the bully
- Agree, if possible on values and behaviours for the future

→ It is preferable that nothing is put in writing at this stage

6

Initial Responses: Best Practice for Managers

Chapter outline
Initial Responses:
Best Practice for Managers

→ Listening with empathy
→ Useful forms of words to use
→ Keeping the process informal
→ Coaching the victim to address the issues
   with the alleged perpetrator
→ Exploring agreement on a way forward
→ Mediation

Introduction

This chapter will cover the important issues around how Line Managers and HR professionals should respond to complaints about bullying behaviour. The responses that will be treated are all aimed at trying to resolve the matter as effectively as possible, as close to the source as possible and with as little 'red tape' or bureaucracy as possible.

The manager who first hears about a bullying and/or harassment claim should immediately stop all other processes that are in train, if any, in respect of that individual. For example if there is a disciplinary process in progress then it must stop while the B&H claim is treated at local level, mediated or investigated.

The responding manager must listen with significant empathy and caring to the issues raised by the individual without in any way leaving the impression with the claimant that the claim is proven just because it is being spoken about. Notwithstanding this, it is important that the responding manager and the organisation attach importance to the predicament in which the recipient sees herself/himself.

Every effort should be made to maintain as much informality in the system as is possible. Thus if it is possible to prevent any formal complaints being made then that certainly would be preferable for all concerned, as one would have a better chance of resolving an issue at the informal stage. Ensure that you explain the way you intend to proceed in the informal process.

Panel 6.1

Key behavioural steps for a manager when faced with a B&H complaint

→ Stop all processes that are in train

→ Listen with empathy and caring

→ Keep the process as informal as possible

→ Preferably take no notes during early meetings — just listen intently. It may be prudent to make some contemporaneous notes, dated, after the meeting recalling what occurred

→ Empower and coach the individual to address his/her concerns to the alleged perpetrator, if at all possible

→ Encourage employee to explore agreement with the alleged perpetrator on an acceptable way forward

→ Stress need for confidentiality

Panel 6.2

Useful forms of words to maintain an informal approach

→ 'You have identified an issue, I'm listening, tell me what happened. Take your time. I won't be taking formal notes today; I just want to explore the issue to see if it is possible to find a resolution that is acceptable. If not, there is always the formal grievance and disciplinary process which I am sure you are familiar with. Yes? I have a copy of the B&H Grievance Policy and the Dignity at Work policy here for you. Let me explain to you the informal and formal process and possible next steps for you if we can't find a solution here

→ I will ask the respondent in a separate meeting to explain his/her perspective on this same issue

→ Once I have heard both sides, I will meet with you both either separately or together to see what potential there is for a local informal solution

→ Are you comfortable to proceed in this way as an interim approach?

A clear manifestation of this informality would be that the listening manager would not in fact take any notes as these may be evidence as such and may need to be clarified with the complainant and then formally passed to the respondent.

Once one has understood the position of the claimant one should explore the possibility of moving into a solution-oriented mode. Some individuals may initially be reluctant to get into such a mode, based on the degree of pain that they are feeling at that particular time. Thus it may be beneficial to spend some time discussing such an initiative even if the meeting is to be adjourned for some hours/days.

Once the individual has agreed to adopt a solution-oriented mode the manager should point out that the really best way of proceeding is to examine whether or not the individual could discuss his/her concerns directly with the person who in their view is behaving badly towards them.

This is a critically important part of the process. If successfully carried out, not alone has one a better chance of a successful resolution but in most instances the individual will feel all the better for having taken this kind of initiative themselves.

The complainant may need some help in developing a positive attitude towards this kind of initiative and also with the development of the skills required to bring this off. There is no rocket science in this and it should be possible in most situations to bring even an individual who is not naturally very assertive to a point whereby they can go through with such an initiative and derive the benefits therefrom.

If the individual does get to the point where they feel that they can approach the alleged perpetrator in this way, then it is important that they follow some of the advice earlier given in Chapter 4 and summarised in Panels 4.1 and 4.2.

It is important to be aware that the alleged perpetrator may feel that he/she is the 'victim'. In their view all they were doing was trying to improve the job performance of the complainant; they now feel that, as a consequence, the tables are being turned on them.

Panel 6.3

Ways of helping the complainant to talk directly with the alleged perpetrator

→ Explain that it is decidedly the best option for resolution

→ Influence the individual to seeing that they are likely to personally get to a better place if they themselves address their concerns directly to the perpetrator

→ Highlight some of the more difficult aspects of Mediation and particularly Investigation

→ Explore whether or not there is another trusted one with whom the complainant could discuss the options

→ Explain the support or skill development that the individual might require for their interaction with the alleged perpetrator

A final insight for managers who become involved in attempts to resolve B&H situations is that they must maintain total confidentiality about all aspects of the case. The most helpful behaviour for those directly involved as accuser and accused is that unhelpful talk around the organisation is kept to an absolute minimum.

If the parties cannot resolve the grievance between themselves, and they are both willing to work at and seek a confidential solution, then mediation is best. With the assistance of a trained interventionist – internal or external – the parties in the dispute may arrive at a working agreement on how to behave towards each other in the future and accept and resolve the issue in dispute.

It is to this subject of Mediation that we now turn in Chapter 7

Summary of Chapter 6

→ Initial responses to a Bullying and Harassment complaint can greatly aid resolution

→ All HR processes in train in respect of an employee should stop once a Bullying and Harassment complaint is made

→ The responding manager must listen with empathy

→ Keep the process as informal as possible

→ Preferably take no notes, as they are likely to make settlement more difficult

→ Empower individual to address his/her concerns to the perpetrator and provide coaching and support for this

→ Encourage the parties to explore agreement on values and behaviours for the future

→ Help the parties to maintain a solution-oriented mode

→ Confidentiality must be maintained

→ Mediation is the best course if the parties cannot agree between themselves

Mediation Processes

7

Chapter outline
Mediation Processes

→ Agreement on a mediator
→ Terms of Reference
→ Skills of a good mediator
→ Sample Mediation process
→ Building trust
→ Searching for common ground
→ Agreeing Values and acceptable on-going behaviours
→ Review of on-going relationships

Introduction

Many organisations provide for the mediation of more difficult B&H claims that have not been amenable to resolution at the local level or the other processes outlined in the previous chapter. Some of these organisations train internal mediators and a particular mediator is usually agreed between the parties who have the disagreement. Alternatively those organisations which have not trained individuals as mediators or where issues are of a sufficiently difficult nature may well go outside to look for an experienced and skilled mediator.

In either of the above situations mediation should be seen as the first semi-formal approach to resolving the issues between the individuals. We say semi-formal insofar as once one has passed from the truly informal local stage one arrives at this stage where there is an increase in the degree of formality; however, this level of formality is nowhere near the formality of a full investigation, the subject of our next chapter.

When using an external mediator it is usual that the parties will also have to agree on the appointment of a particular individual in their case. Normal practice here is that organisations usually have access to a number of mediators and they propose she/he whom they regard as the most suitable for the particular case with each of the individuals hopefully subscribing their agreement.

Failing immediate agreement on the nominated mediator a consultation process would continue until a mediator agreeable to all sides would be appointed.

The terms of reference need to be agreed between the organisation and the mediator. This task is usually undertaken by the manager within the organisation charged with trying to bring the matter to a satisfactory conclusion. It could for example be the manager of the complainant or the respondent, or alternatively it could be the HR Manager. The substantive task for such a person is to write to the mediator requesting them to mediate, delineating some of the parameters around the mediation and perhaps passing to the mediator relevant internal policies, such as the Dignity at Work Policy.

Panel 7.1

Skills of a good mediator

→ Experienced in handling B&H mediations

→ Good attending skills – focus, impartiality, caring and withholding judgement

→ Strong listening skills

→ Good questioning skills – consistent across all interviews

→ Skilled in conflict diagnosis, analysis and resolution

→ Good consensus building skills, including re-framing techniques

→ Ability to look at the total picture and help the parties to do likewise

The next stage of the process should see the agreed Mediator sharing with the principals the process and procedures that he/she proposes to use. The mediator may be required to modify his/her normal process depending on particular nuances that exist in an individual case; in addition there may be some negotiation around the fringes to satisfy particular viewpoints about the process that may be held by either party.

In some situations it may be appropriate to provide a formal pre-mediation agreement that would include such items as roles, dispositions of the parties, process, confidentiality and clarity about nothing said at mediation being able to be raised in any court action.

In addition the 'non-discussables' or non-disclosables that are told to the mediator by either party in their first meeting — the pre-mediation meeting — should be agreed and adhered to throughout the process. A mediator upon hearing both sides, will make a determination on whether this dispute is mediatable or not and will withdraw in a situation where, if for example, they feel that either party is not fully committed to the process.

It is usual that the mediator will talk with each of the main characters in the dispute commencing with the claimant. The first task during this consultation is to establish what is the unacceptable behaviour in the view of the complainant and how regularly this behaviour is occurring along with the resultant feelings within the claimant. The Mediator should be at pains to let the claimant clearly see that she/he fully understands the situation; he/she should put in place whatever checking mechanisms are available so as to ensure that the claimant is confident that their situation has been fully 'heard'.

The mediator will then go through a similar process with the respondent again taking pains to clearly understand the respondent's view of their behaviour towards the claimant.

In these meetings with both parties the Mediator should make strenuous efforts to build trust with the parties as this is one of the principal building blocks for a potential settlement. The disputing parties will develop this trust if the Mediator adopts a caring, understanding mode and clearly appears not to take sides in the listening part of his/her data gathering.

It is preferable that the mediator not 'carry messages' between claimant and respondent. Hopefully the mediator will be able to ultimately create a climate where each of these individuals will be able to address the issues at hand and their feelings during later

Panel 7.2

Sample Mediation Process

→ The mediator(s) will meet separately with both parties for pre-mediation meetings, gather a brief outline of the complaint and response, clarify the process and terms of engagement, explain the ground rules and other alternative approaches available to the parties should mediation not succeed

→ It is important that parties understand that they are responsible for the solutions derived at in mediation and that coming to such solutions will be within their control, but will be facilitated by a skilled mediator

→ The mediator should clarify what is confidential in the issues discussed to ensure that those issues are not transferred in discussions with the other party

→ The mediator will then meet with both parties simultaneously so as to briefly outline the process that will be used for this mediation and to take any further

questions of clarification concerning process

→ The Mediator will then meet separately with the parties, listen to and fully understand their issues; he/she will provide opportunity to each individual to check that he has correctly heard their issues

→ The Mediator will help the parties to clarify one another's issues to the extent that they can at least understand where the other person is coming from; this part of the process will initially involve individual meetings but may quickly/slowly get to clarifying these issues in a joint meeting between the Mediator and both parties.

→ The parties, with the help of the Mediator, will attempt to identify some values and future behaviours that each would find acceptable from one another and hopefully move towards a 'solution' that builds on some common ground and is focussed on the way in which each of the parties should treat one another in the weeks/months/years ahead

→ If this future-oriented solution is mutually acceptable the parties would need to work with the Mediator to:

ⓐ Anticipate roadblocks and find ways around same, and

ⓑ Put in place the enabling conditions for the success of the new arrangements

→ The parties would also need to put in place review mechanisms whereby they themselves could monitor progress with the outcomes above; some assistance may be required from the Mediator in the early phases of these reviews and from line management in the latter phases

The above outline is just that, an outline. The parties would need to invest sufficient credibility in the mediator's experience and skill that they can accept that she/he may well deviate from the above if circumstances warrant such a move.

face-to-face meetings rather than have the messages transmitted as it were by a messenger.

The next important phase for the mediator is to develop the bones of a way forward from what emerges, as it were, from the 'stories' of the complainant and the respondent. At these meetings (or later ones) the mediator is likely to propose some values to which both sides could subscribe and to develop these further into some specific behaviours that would give expression to these values. In so doing the mediator should look for behaviours around particular flash points that may have been occurring between the individuals. We have earlier shown a sample set of such Values and Behaviours in Panel 5.2 within Chapter 5.

Once the mediator has achieved his/her own clarity about these values and behaviours it will be necessary to perhaps initially discuss them with each of the parties. In other cases he/she may decide that the first airing of these values/behaviours will be with both parties present. The particular advantage of doing it individually is that the mediator is able to gauge perhaps more accurately how both individuals will respond to these values beyond the meeting when they are back in the real world within the organisation.

If the mediator has discussed these values separately and has seen a clear understanding of them within the two individuals and, perhaps more importantly, a commitment to living these values and behaviours in their daily interaction at work then it may be close to 'sign-up' time — the time when both parties commit fully to working together with full dignity and respect being afforded by both sides.

Most competent mediators will also establish some review mechanism to monitor progress in the weeks/months ahead. It is not unusual for one or two of these review meetings to be chaired by the mediator who would want to hear from each individual how the intervening period has gone. This review process would then be passed back to the relevant line manager who would carry out subsequent periodic reviews in a supportive manner.

Following several successful reviews it would be safe to say that the mediation would appear to have been successful. However sometimes events can occur that push the settlement off the rails. In the case of any such flare-up it is important to get the parties back talking directly about the issues or back into mediation.

In some situations either prior to mediation or post a failed mediation it may be necessary to consider a formal Investigation and it is to this process that we turn in the next Chapter.

Summary of Chapter 7

→ Mediation should be the first recourse after local resolution efforts — it offers the best semi-formal opportunity for progress

→ The mediator to be used is usually agreed by the parties to the dispute as in his/her terms of reference

→ The mediator should ensure that the process to be used is agreed at the first meeting

→ The mediator talks separately with each side so as to understand each set of issues

→ Mediators should strive to build trust and not 'carry messages' from one party to the other

→ The mediator should then look for common ground where he/she can build towards improved behaviour between the parties

→ Mediator should strive to agree values/behaviours for the on-going relationship of the parties

→ A monitoring and review mechanism should be agreed prior to the end of the mediation

Formal Investigations

8

Chapter outline
Formal Investigations

→ Appointment of Investigator
→ Structure of an Investigation
→ Sample Investigation procedure
→ Investigation tips for complainants
→ Investigation tips for respondents
→ Representation
→ Role of Investigation Manager

Panel 8.1

Sample Structure of an investigation:

➊ Pre Work

→ Employer to forward complaint, response and all relevant policies to the proposed Investigator(s) for consideration, suitability & availability

→ Forward Investigators credentials to parties/unions for objections. If no objections – appoint Investigator

→ Issue for (if employer determining TOR) or Investigator to arrange to meet with parties and their representatives to agree the Terms of Reference

→ Forward all relevant paperwork to all parties and schedule interviews

➋ Investigation

→ Meet complainant to gather full evidence on grievance

→ Meet respondent(s) to gather full response

→ Meet witnesses. Confidential minutes taken. Recommend a note taker – independent

→ Issue minutes. (Ensure clarity around the process for this – eg time frames, disputes)

→ Agreed minutes forwarded to complainant and respondent(s) in batches throughout investigation

→ Gather evidence throughout

→ Meet respondents and complainant close to end of process to give them the opportunity to respond to any issues raised in the minutes or the process

➌ Reporting

→ Review all minutes and evidence

→ Compile relevant appendices

→ Write report

→ Issue report

Panel 8.2

Sample Investigation Procedure

→ All parties to the dispute will be offered the opportunity of making written submissions to the Investigator, who can be contacted at... These written submissions may often be already made by the time an organisation decides to investigate the issue. They will be forwarded to the Investigator with a letter of appointment and the agreed terms of reference

→ In many grievance investigations, most organisations determine the Terms of Reference — i.e. what they want investigated (internally or externally). However, in a Dignity at Work investigation — it is common practice for the parties to agree the terms of reference — which sets out the scope of the investigation

→ All parties will be offered the opportunity of presenting their case/ views at a private Hearing with the Investigator who will seek clarification on core and peripheral issues as they arise. Specific assertions made by one party will be shared with the other claimant(s)/respondent(s) as appropriate. At the end of such a Hearing the claimant(s)/respondent(s) will be required to summarise their position(s) if they have not already done so in writing

→ The Investigator may propose for agreement by the parties that the situation requires a joint Hearing wherein the claimant(s)/respondent(s) will have opportunity to confront relevant issues in the presence of each other; questions of clarification and cross-examination may be pursued by either party. At the end of such a Hearing the claimant(s)/ respondent(s) will be required to summarise their position(s)

→ The Investigator should agree how the meetings will be recorded

→ Each party will have an opportunity to suggest relevant witnesses who will be interviewed in private by the Investigator; in certain limited circumstances cross-examination of these witnesses may be permitted. Alternatively the parties will receive a copy of all the signed minutes in advance of the compilation of a report in order to give them a chance to respond to the comments made in the minutes

→ The Investigator may decide to interview other relevant parties who may/may not have been mentioned within the Hearings or within the documentation on the basis that said individuals may have information that could throw light on the viewpoints of the claimant(s)/respondent(s)

→ Any party may, if he/she so wishes, be accompanied by their trade union representative or by a colleague at any stage of this Investigation. If both parties are represented by the same union it is not considered good practice from a confidentiality perspective for the same person to accompany both the complainant and respondent in a case

→ Meetings should be minuted and the minutes agreed and signed off by all those interviewed prior to being issued to any party in the case

→ Having met all the witnesses, the Investigator would normally meet both the complainant and respondent again separately to challenge, verify or validate any evidence from the witnesses in advance of commencing the production of the investigation analysis and report

→ Following the Hearings the Investigator will take a period of reflection of some days or weeks depending on the body of evidence, prior to issuing a Determination in writing

meetings, once agreed. Likewise if the respondent puts a response in writing it should also be shared with the claimant and equally so too should their agreed minutes be shared. Sufficient time should elapse between the exchange of these documents and the first formal investigation

Panel 8.3

Investigation tips for complainants

→ Prepare well

→ Describe the incident(s) in sequence

→ List any facts, witnesses, dates or times that support your recall of the incident(s)

→ Let the Investigator know the feelings that the incident(s) has/have left you with

→ Explain the context of the instances

→ Explain any attempts made to resolve the issue(s)

→ Indicate how you feel the matter should be resolved

→ Answer all questions honestly

meeting to allow for the parties' full consideration and possible responses to the documentation.

If the complainant has not put any thoughts in writing the Investigator should encourage them to do so in a brief document which they should write in language that is as non-emotive as possible. This document should then be given to the other party who should feel free to put their response into writing – again this should be shared with the other party.

Representation should be offered to both parties who should be free to bring to an investigation whatever representative they believe can be most helpful to them. In most instances these representatives are not only there as silent support but take a full part in aiding the case of the individual they are representing.

Most Investigators will conduct separate hearings of the complainant and respondent cases, usually taking the complainant case first. Then interviewing the respondent(s), then any witnesses and finally the complainant and respondent again.

It may be necessary to re-hear the case of both complainant and respondent as the investigation proceeds depending on the evidence surfaced.

Panel 8.4

Investigation tips for respondents

→ Prepare well

→ Focus on the complained of behaviours and give your responses specifically to those incidents complained of

→ Explain the context and any subsequent events that may be relevant

→ Paint a picture as fully as possible of your demeanour at the time of the alleged incidents

→ Use all available support documentation and witnesses where applicable

→ Bring any diaries and or contemporaneous notes to the meeting

→ Clarify what you had hoped to achieve in the situation(s) complained of

→ Answer all questions honestly

→ Be aware that you are most likely being met after the complainant and the Investigator may discuss issues that were not in the written complaint but mentioned at the complaint meeting; you may have to revert to them with information they request in relation to these 'new issues'. The evidence is based on the complaint (written or not) and evidence gathered at meetings. The same principle applies to you. It is an attempt to afford parties to a dispute the right to expand and explain the complaint, based on the principle that a party should not be limited in their right to make a complaint by their inability or not to write a complaint

The Investigator should also hear the witnesses that are nominated by either party or others, who may not have been nominated but who, in the opinion of the Investigator, may have some information that is material to the investigation. Witnesses need to be handled delicately as some find it difficult to function well in these formal investigations where they themselves may even feel that they are 'on trial'. Others, while clearly wanting to give evidence in support of the party that nominated them, find it difficult to be speaking against another employee, as it were. Sensitive handling of such witnesses by the Investigator will lead to more productive sessions. It is not usual for witnesses to be represented at B&H Investigations. However, many dignity at work policies facilitate witnesses having a support person with them, and at the start of each meeting it is explained that their role is support and not representative – they cannot answer the questions for the witness. A statement to that effect is signed by them and returned to the Investigator or investigation team.

A situation sometimes arises whereby an individual complainant or respondent is on sick leave at the time when the investigation should be proceeding. In such a situation the organisation needs to take a caring approach and may need to distinguish as to whether or not the individual is unfit for work or unfit to partake in the process. Sometimes one finds that an individual who is unfit for work may well be both willing and able to partake in the process.

Panel 8.5

Sample Appointment of Investigator and Terms of Reference letter

Dear X

I would be very pleased if you would accept the role of Investigator in a B&H dispute where 'A' has made certain assertions about 'B'.

It is my understanding that you will:
- Hear both sides
- Allow full representation of each individual
- Hear any witnesses proposed by either party

At the conclusion of your investigation you should provide a written Determination, which should be simultaneously forwarded to the claimant, the respondent and to me as Investigation Manager.

You will have full access to all relevant documentation and any other staff, if necessary.

Yours etc.

However, if proceeding in such a scenario, one does need to ask questions about whether or not this would create or add to stress for the individual; if there is any real possibility of this, then the investigation should not go ahead at this time.

It would be remiss to conclude this chapter without making reference to the position of alleged perpetrators, who may oftentimes be accused in the wrong. This can arise in situations where a staff member of such a manager is having difficulties in one or more of the areas below:

→ Inability to meet reasonable targets

→ Persistent poor performance

→ Poor attendance and/or timekeeping

→ Lack of teamwork

Some managers who genuinely try to turn around some of these situations – whether through counselling or in the formal disciplinary process – may find that the tables are then turned by the submission of a complaint of harassment.

It is important in such situations that the rights of such managers are protected, just as we have earlier advocated strongly for the rights of natural justice to be fully respected for complainants and respondents alike. Such complaints must be fully investigated, affording all due rights to all parties.

Once the Investigator has heard the positions of each of the parties, their representatives and their witnesses he/she will usually take some time to consider the case before pronouncing judgement; the Determination of the Investigator should be simultaneously passed to the complainant, respondent and the organisation.

As a final note many organisations appoint an Investigation Manager who will manage the process of the appointment of an Investigator, the agreement of the parties to same, the terms of reference and any other administrative matters that need to be attended to during the investigation, such as the calling of witnesses.

Account may have to be taken within this Determination of the fact that the parties may no longer be able to work together; in such an eventuality, the organisation will be required to seek alternative working arrangements.

More formal external institutional and legal avenues are available for the more intractable cases. These institutional Tribunals or Investigators process B&H grievances along similar lines to that which is outlined above but on a decidedly more formal and now public basis. The same can be said for utilising civil court procedures insofar as they become very public and carry even more onerous responsibilities for any witnesses that may be called to such a forum.

All of that which has been written in this chapter, particularly that relating to external investigations, re-emphasises the point that has earlier been made on a couple of occasions – one should utilise local and/or mediation processes to the fullest extent possible in endeavouring to resolve B&H conflicts.

Summary of Chapter 8

→ The individual Investigator is usually agreed between the parties

→ The organisation should clarify terms of reference at the time of appointing the Investigator

→ The Investigator should agree with the parties the process to be used in the investigation

→ The Investigator should meet in turn the complainant, respondent and witnesses where applicable

→ Complainant and respondent should be offered representation and witnesses can be accompanied

→ On occasions an Investigation may revert to the mediation process, if the Investigator feels this would be fruitful

→ Following a short period of reflection the Investigator will issue a Determination

Best Practice Procedures

9

Chapter outline
Best Practice Procedures

→ The 7 Ps
→ Having the right Policies in place
→ Clear Procedures for grievance and dignity at work
→ Good Protocols in place to aid conflict resolution
→ Sound Organisation Practices
→ People should be at the core of processes
→ Places chosen to provide for privacy
→ Prevention tools for manager

Introduction

Once a complaint of Bullying and Harassment has been lodged it absorbs:

→ Extensive soul searching on behalf of the complainant

→ Similar soul searching from the respondent, and

→ Extensive management time and effort

A clear agreed set of organisation policies and procedures are both a psychological, legal and productivity comfort to complainants, respondents and organisations. At a minimum they save time in disagreements in interpretation. More importantly they ensure a consistent, standard and fair approach that shapes the process – the 'how to' and 'what to' - and set the expectations for complainant, respondent, witnesses, management, union and any other party involved in the complaint.

If a management team finds itself defending actions in a particular grievance or complaint in an external agency or in court, little allowance will be afforded them for having poor policies or procedures.

The development of good Policies and Procedures is a planned activity and the time invested in them in the early stages can save money, time and effort in retrospectively writing policies that fit the problems that emerge and don't account for future problems.

Best Practice Guidelines: *The 7 Ps*

Organisations endeavouring to ensure a culture free of bullying and harassment should evaluate the work they have done in the following seven areas.

1. **Policies**
2. **Procedures**
3. **Protocols**
4. **Practices**
5. **People**
6. **Places**
7. **Prevention**

Put these **7Ps** in place and as an organisation you are better positioned to deal with a B&H complaint. You will minimise the time, energy and resources internal managers need to spend in dealing with it and should it not be resolved internally, you are better placed to defend it, externally.

1. Policies:
Informal or Formal:

As individuals look at an organisation's policies they should be able to see an informal and a formal route. Our best advice is

→ Keep it as informal as possible

→ Resolve locally

→ Mediate

Such an informal approach offers the best chance of low level, local resolution with as little damage a possible to the parties involved.

If someone presents to you as a manager, team leader or HR executive with a B&H complaint you must determine whether it is possible to:

→ Preferably proceed along the lines above, or

→ Proceed to a formal investigation

In the context that for most disputes the informal should be appropriate, one should note the advantages/disadvantages of each approach as shown within the 'Pros and Cons' presented within Panel 9.1 below.

❷ Procedures

Every organisation should have a clearly stated Grievance and Dignity at Work policy, up to date and accessible to all employees. Within Panel 9.2 and 9.3 overleaf we present sample policies in respect of Grievance and Dignity at Work.

Panel 9.1

Pros & Cons: Informal & Formal

Informal		Formal	
Pro	Con	Pro	Con
Early resolution	May not resolve it	Determination made	May not resolve it
Parties own the solution	May fester	Surfaces evidence	May surface too much
Resolved close to source	Parties may not be interested in this route	Thorough & Fair	Involves many parties — witnesses
Fast	Confidential	Public — Written report	Can be long running

Panel 9.2

Sample Employee Grievance Procedure

This organisation is committed to maintaining excellent communication with all staff. It is hoped that these communication practices will ensure that all employee grievances are heard and acted upon.

Employees who feel the need to further process a grievance should:

→ Take their grievance in the first instance to their immediate team leader/manager

→ If the grievance is not resolved at the above stage the aggrieved employee should then take their grievance to the next level; every effort should be made to resolve the employee's grievance through collaboration between this manager, the team member's manager and the aggrieved person themselves

→ Failure to resolve the grievance at the above stage will provide the aggrieved employee with the opportunity of processing their grievance to the next level of management, to HR or to the CEO; the manager at this level will again strive to work with the relevant parties to solve the grievance in as speedy a manner as possible

→ The aggrieved employee has the opportunity at any of the stages above of processing their grievance through their Union representative, if applicable

❸ Protocols

Clearly defined protocols, procedures that are fair and transparent are essential for a culture of openness to prevail.

The process for making and processing a claim should be confidential, non-prohibitive and non-victimising of the complainant or potential respondent.

Organisations should endeavour to have protocols in place for the eventualities within Panel 9.3, opposite.

Five of these protocols have already been described in this

Panel 9.3

Sample Dignity at Work

The Board and Senior Management commit to:

→ Actively creating a climate that fully respects the individual at all times

→ Ensuring that no Bullying, Harassment or Sexual Harassment is tolerated under any circumstances

→ Conducting workshops to ensure that all employees are fully aware of this policy and of the recourse that they have should they feel that this policy is being breached

Employees are please asked to note that the following procedure is available to them in the event of any breach of the Dignity at Work policy:

→ The employee, if they feel able, should in the first instance indicate to the relevant individual that his/her behaviour is unacceptable and the reasons why this is so

→ If the undesired behaviour does not cease the complainant should go to a more senior individual or one of the specifically nominated individuals in the organisation and inform them of the breach

→ The complainant at this stage has the option of a mediated solution being pursued or of proceeding to a formal investigation, where they can be represented

→ None of the above takes from the employee having the right to take this complaint to an outside Agency

This Dignity at Work policy becomes effect from

....

book (a, b, c, d, f below) and the remaining three, the protocol for opening a B&H meeting (e), a protocol for issuing of findings & report (g) and the protocol for appeal (h) are shown right and opposite.

Panel 9.4

Sample B & H Protocols

ⓐ Protocol for handling a complaint. Ref. Panel 6.1 Page. 47

ⓑ Protocol for Agreeing Terms of Reference. Ref Panel 8.5 Page. 68

ⓒ Protocol for agreeing Investigator. Ref. Page 63

ⓓ Protocol for structure of Investigation. Ref. Panel 8.1 Page. 63

ⓔ Protocol for opening at a formal B & H meeting

ⓕ Protocol on Procedure of Investigation. Ref. Panel 8.2 Page. 64 & 65

ⓖ Protocol for issuing of Findings & Report

ⓗ Protocol for appeal.

Protocol **ⓖ** :
Procedure for issuing of Findings and Report

The Investigator should be issued with a procedure for issuing their final report and at the terms of reference stage an estimated time frame for the completion of the report might be agreed.

The instruction could read:

....

The Investigator will produce a report on their findings and recommendations in a timely manner. It should include details on the brief given and Terms of Reference of the Investigation. It should explain the policies and procedures applied in the investigation and list the incidents complained of. The facts established for each of the incidents should be clearly stated. The Investigator should make a Determination on each incident based on the facts established. The Conclusions or the complaint should be clearly stated and any recommendations made should be relevant to the issues raised and within the power and scope of the organisation to implement. All appendices referred to should be attached to the final report or appendixed in a separate report if the final report size is prohibitive. The Report should be presented to the investigating manager or HR manager, signed and dated by the Investigator.

Protocol ⓗ: Appeal

If your organisation allows the right of an appeal after an investigation — internal or external, then it should have a protocol for appeal.

Organisations should strive to ensure that consistency is achieved between what it says on paper (the policies) and behaviour (the practices). It should 'do what it says on the tin!'

A sample appeal protocol is listed below.

→ The complainant and the person complained against will have the right to appeal the decision to the nominated officer of the Company, usually Head of HR, MD or CEO — depending on the organisation structure

→ The Appeal should be made in writing within a specific timeframe, usually 14-28 days

→ The Appeal should state the specific reasons for appealing the decision

→ Following the Consideration of the Appeal which may involve a hearing, the appointed officer will inform the person who made the appeal whether or not they have upheld the Appeal

→ They should be advised of any proposed action that will taken

❹ Practices

The culture for surfacing the issue of potential Bullying or Harassment (as evidenced by behaviour and practices) should be open and accessible. What an organisation states on paper in it's policies, procedures or protocols and what actually gets done in practice can sometimes be different.

Organisations should strive to ensure that consistency is achieved between what it says on paper (the policies) and behaviour (the practices). It should 'do what it says on the tin!'

❺ People

People are core to business. People are important. It is always people that are involved in a grievance - we have never investigated a

Panel 9.5

Protocol **e**:
Opening a B&H Meeting – Formal

1. Welcome ☐

2. Names of Investigators and Roles ☐

3. Your role here is as Witness/Complainant/Respondent ☐

4. Terms of Reference – Show & Accept Scope to Proceed ☐

5. List Policy(ies) being investigated under – Grievance/Dignity at Work ☐

6. Our/My job is to investigate facts {Credibility or otherwise truth of allegations} ☐

7. Right to be accompanied. Advise Union Rep/Friend of role – support or Representative – policy dependent ☐

8. Strictly Confidential; Failure to comply with confidentiality may result in disciplinary action ☐

9. Describe the Process of Recording Minutes ☐
   - Minutes of Meeting signed & keep one copy.
   - Minutes available to complainant and the respondent
   - If changes required
   - If in Dispute - describe options
   - From Date of Issue they must be returned signed as agreed within X days else deemed agreed.
   - Credibility of Witnesses may be relied upon to form an opinion.

10. Reserve the Right to meet again ☐

11. Report Compiled {Action upheld or not upheld} ☐

12. Explain the process - more detail in the report ☐

13. Staff Support Services Available ☐

14. Both parties have risk of adverse findings & both have rights of natural justice ☐

15. Items available to us{what investigators have access to} ☐

16. Will be treated fairly in the process – recess/break any time you require it ☐

17. Right to revert to mediation in this process if all parties accept such an option ☐

18. Have our/my full attention ☐

19. Any Questions? ☐

machine for B&H! People need the respect of having their grievance taken seriously – whether it is eventually upheld or not.

People manage and lead people every day in organisations. People who are distracted from their core business – engineering, production, sales, administration, etc – by conflict and grievances will not be as productive as those that are not. Give people the tools to effectively handle conflict in all walks of organisational life.

Conflict is natural in organisations but people are not always 'natural' in handling conflict.

Conflict is natural in organisations but people are not always 'natural' in handling conflict, whether they are embroiled in it or attempting to resolve it from a team leading or management perspective. Make your business centred around the people that work in it, keep in touch with them, see their challenges and difficulties and ensure to treat all grievances and complaints as quickly, consistently and as locally as possible. The prompt attention that you give the employee with the difficulty will be appreciated by them, whether the difficulty eventually goes away or becomes a formal B&H case.

❻ Places:
The Physical settings:

It is important to have the right physical settings to uphold best practice. If a complaint is made and the complainant wants to discuss it privately with HR or their union, this should be facilitated. A private meeting room – inside or outside the building should be made available.

Electronic booking systems should not list it as a grievance or complaint meeting or cite the parties' names. It could be generically booked in their department's name or in the name of HR. This room should be out of the general eye and ear shot of colleagues that may be aware of the on-going tensions and may take the cue by the meeting that something is wrong. Instead book the meeting room on another floor, if that is possible or in HR, if it is private. The room should have natural light if possible. Some paper and pens should be available in addition to some water – no stimulants like tea or coffee or soft drinks. The room should have a table and chairs and a box of tissues.

❼ Prevention:
Training & Awareness

Prevention is better than cure. Train your people in effective management techniques and keep it as internal and local as possible by training up internal people in mediation skills and cultural diversity training.

A core group of internal people could be trained and skilled in mediation techniques to ensure that all conflicts are dealt with as quickly and effectively as possible, without reliance on the availability of external experts.

Providing Diversity and Interpersonal Awareness training, Conflict Diagnosis and Resolution Training for those in team leading or management positions may help to resolve the small conflicts that can arise daily and large ones intermittently.

Ensure that all management are trained in key areas including:

→ Best Practice Management Techniques

→ Interpersonal Effectiveness

→ Conflict Diagnosis and Resolution

→ Mediation Skills

→ Communication Skills

→ General Principles of HR

Good training allows your management to be ready and enabled to apply common sense, best practice policies, protocols and procedures to complaints as they arise and to prevent many of them surfacing by fostering a culture of Dignity at Work, which is discussed further in Chapter 10.

Summary of Chapter 9

→ Remember to put the 7 Ps in place in your organisation

→ **Policies:** Be sure that good policies exist for informal and formal resolution efforts

→ **Procedures:** Every organisation should have clear and accessible Grievance and Dignity at Work procedures

→ **Protocols:** Having good protocols in place greatly aids conflict resolution

→ **Practices:** Organisations should ensure that response behaviours are consistent with policies

→ **People:** Staff are at the core of an organisation's business processes and should always be treated with dignity

→ **Places:** Privacy should be provided for conflict resolution efforts

→ **Prevention:** Provide management and staff with appropriate training and development in respect of resolving organisational conflict

Establishing a Culture of Dignity at Work

10

Chapter outline
Establishing a Culture of
Dignity at Work

→   Role of Senior Management in making
    Dignity and Respect a priority
→   Focus on values
→   Sample set of Values/Behaviours
→   Putting the enabling conditions in place
→   Workshops
→   Celebrating Diversity

Introduction

In the earlier part of this book we emphasised the need for organisations to seriously set about establishing a culture of dignity at work and we would like to address this issue in greater detail at this juncture.

Many organisations in recent years have taken a values approach to the way in which it wishes to motivate employees to certain behaviours within their organisation. Some of these organisations have produced excellent value statements but have left them to rot in the nice frames in which they are placed

The role of senior management is critical in driving the values and behaviours throughout the workplace.

at strategic locations throughout the organisation. Other organisations have taken the creation of a value set as the first step to inculcating those values into the daily work of the organisation; they have searched assiduously for specific behaviours that individuals can engage in to bring these values alive.

The latter approach needs to be taken within organisations in respect of dignity and respect (D&R) at work. The organisation needs to focus on the values that it would have around dignity at work and to test those at a variety of levels in the organisation prior to formal adoption by the senior management team. Once adopted

it will be important for managers at all levels in the organisation to manage behaviour consistent with these values, behaviour that enriches the living organisation's view of dignity and respect at work.

The role of senior management is critical in driving the values and behaviours throughout the workplace. They must take their task sufficiently seriously that they will, in collaboration with their colleagues, put in place the 'enabling' conditions for the living of the agreed values and behaviours at all levels. This implies that they will work with their management colleagues to identify appropriate supports for D&R behaviour at succeeding levels within the organisation.

The organisation must also use its best expertise to put together policies and practices that flow from the above values and it will be the responsibility of line management to ensure compliance with these policies. This can be aided by adding some time to business meetings such as production, sales and other meetings within the organisation in order to discuss aspects of the policies and practices as applied to that particular unit of the organisation. Oftentimes such behaviour is more beneficial than formal workshops/training courses on dignity although these have a place within a multifaceted approach to dignity.

Panel 10.1

Sample set of key organisational values/ behaviours in respect of dignity at work

Values	Behaviours
Always treat the other with D&R	All staff will be proactively encouraged to treat others with the D&R that they themselves expect to receive.
Inclusive Communication	Staff at all levels will be afforded optimum inclusive communication so as to ensure that all relevant job/organisation information is available to them in a timely manner.
Performance Feedback	All staff will be provided with opportunities to discuss performance feedback on four occasions each year; this will be a key result area for all managers.
Personal Development	Personal development will be the subject of a separate action-oriented meeting between Team Leaders and each team member on two occasions per year.
Organisational Commitment	The Senior Management Team (and subsequently each manager) will audit D&R Values and Behaviours within their domain twice per year.
Culture for Conflict Management	Conflict is understood by all to be a natural part of change and growth in organisational life; a culture that embraces conflict and encourages staff to be conflict cognisant is embraced by all.

Many organisations have also taken the opportunity to focus on particular minorities in the organisation and have a focus day where some of their culture can be explained by the employees themselves to other employees; such processes are aimed at giving as good an appreciation as possible to others of the positive sides of such minorities.

Panel 10.2

5 steps to culture of dignity

→ Senior Management Team to make D&R a priority

→ Mini-workshops on D&R during normal business meetings

→ 'Insight' workshops for cross-functional groups

→ D&R lived as an ethos in the organisation and not just a charter or policy on the wall

→ Diversity is celebrated and encouraged

Summary of Chapter 10

→ Organisations must establish a culture of Dignity and Respect at work

→ Value statements that are made within such a culture must be brought to life

→ Senior management has a critical role to play in the above

→ Time for discussing Dignity and Respect should be added to normal business meetings

→ Many organisations find ways of celebrating the diversity of their staff

Conclusion

11

Chapter outline
Conclusion

→ Empathy and care
→ Informal mode
→ Local level resolution where possible
→ Best practice at all stages

Conclusion

We have endeavoured to, in the first instance, highlight some typical behaviours of those engaged in B&H; it is our hope that we have demonstrated that an understanding of these behaviours will assist organisations in seeing where the risks are in respect of such B&H activity.

We have been particularly conscious throughout this book to emphasise the empathy and caring with which organisational leaders should respond to those who claim they are being bullied and to those who are accused. This, not to give immediate credence to their version of events, but to allow them explain their issues and their feelings without fear of recrimination.

Thus whenever possible they should maintain as informal a mode as possible and search for a local level resolution.

We have also stressed the urgent need for organisations to create a climate so that those who feel bullied can find their voice. Far too often issues such as B&H have been swept under the carpet or tolerated indefinitely by individuals and the organisation. It is certainly time to treat this issue with the maturity it deserves and encourage all mangers so to do.

We have stressed repeatedly throughout this book the rehabilitative value of equipping the complainant with the frame of mind and behaviour set that allows them address their concerns directly to the individual who is perpetrating the unwanted behaviour. We stress this not alone because such a process has the optimum chance of bringing about a successful resolution; but also because it contributes to freeing the complainant from current and future worry about them not having taken some control of the situation into their own hands.

When we looked at how individual managers should respond to B&H situations that arise in their organisations we stressed the importance of managers getting their initial responses to bullying situations in line with best practice. Thus whenever possible they should maintain as informal a mode as possible and search for a local level resolution that puts the protagonists at ease with one another going forward.

In situations where the local solution for some reason has not worked we have stressed that it is our belief that mediated solutions offer the next best opportunity for a resolution that is mutually satisfactory to complainant and respondent - and which should also be acceptable to the organisation. We have indicated best practice mediation processes and shown that individuals within organisations can be trained as internal mediators. The great benefit of mediation is that it is semi-formal, confidential and control is retained by the parties concerned.

It may be necessary, as a final last resort when as it were all fruit fails, to enter the murky territory of formal investigations. This is usually the next step after mediation attempts have broken down. There are no clear winners in investigations. What investigations do give is a Finding, a Determination of opinion based on the facts as to whether there is

The great benefit of mediation is that it is semi-formal, confidential and control is retained by the parties concerned.

a case to answer or not. Often it is the only resort of long-running or entrenched conflicts that have the potential to proceed to an external legal case. All materials in the investigation are fully discoverable for any further legal proceedings. We really do see that this is a last resort for organisations and we would hope that all forward thinking managers and staff will endeavour to treat it as such.

We hope that you as a manager or a staff member are not too directly confronted by B&H at work or indeed in any other walk of life. If you do come into contact with B&H situations we wish you well in applying some of the basic principles within this book.

Notes